proverbs

proverbs

authorised king james version

printed by authority

published by canongate

with an introduction by | charles johnson

First published in Great Britain in 1998
by Canongate Books Ltd
14 High Street, Edinburgh EH1 1TE

10 9 8 7 6 5 4 3 2

British Library Cataloguing-in-Publication Data
A catalogue record is available on request from
the British Library

ISBN 0 86241 792 9

Typeset by Palimpsest Book Production
Book design by Paddy Cramsie
Printed and bound in Great Britain
by Caledonian International, Bishopbriggs

a note about pocket canons

The Authorised King James Version of the Bible, translated between 1603–11, coincided with an extraordinary flowering of English literature. This version, more than any other, and possibly more than any other work in history, has had an influence in shaping the language we speak and write today. Presenting individual books from the Bible as separate volumes, as they were originally conceived, encourages the reader to approach them as literary works in their own right.

The first twelve books in this series encompass categories as diverse as history, fiction, philosophy, love poetry and law. Each Pocket Canon also has its own introduction, specially commissioned from an impressive range of writers, which provides a personal interpretation of the text and explores its contemporary relevance.

Charles Johnson won the National Book Award in the USA *in 1990 for his novel* Middle Passage. *A widely published literary critic, philosopher, cartoonist, screenwriter, essayist and lecturer, he is one of twelve African-American authors honoured in an international series of stamps celebrating great writers of the twentieth century. He is currently the Pollock Professor of English at the University of Washington. His new novel,* Dreamer, *was published to great acclaim in October 1998.*

introduction by charles johnson

Where there is no vision, the people perish.

Of all the practical observations in that most pragmatic of texts in the Old Testament, *The Book of Proverbs*, this one sentence linking vision and life comes singing off the page as the most profound. Meditate, please, on the possibility that in life there is a *goal*, an end that makes all our worldly efforts intelligible. Carefully think it through: without a *vision*, either personal or political, the individual (or society) is 'like a city that is broken down, and without walls'. This is not simply a question for the schools, for without a comprehensive and capacious philosophy life fails. The unsentimental implication here – the basic, philosophical and secular premise – is that life can be a perilous journey. Perhaps a social minefield. (Just read today's newspaper if you need proof that the world is and has always been a dangerous place.) And any young person hesitantly starting out on this odyssey, now or in the days of King Solomon, soon discovers that his (or her) chances for survival, prosperity and happiness are enhanced a hundred-fold if – and only if – they have a good map.

Put simply, *Proverbs* is that richly detailed, many-splendored map. A timeless wake-up call. More importantly, along with its companion books, the poetic 'wisdom' literature of the Old Testament (*Job, Ecclesiastes, The Song of Solomon,* and *Psalms*), it is a two-millennium-old blue-print for the staggering challenge of living a truly *civilized* life. Culture, we realize after reading *Proverbs*, is an on-going project. We are not born with culture. Or wisdom. And both are but *one* generation deep. Achieving either is a daily task requiring as much work for the individual as an artist puts into a perfectly balanced painting, or a musician into a flawless performance. (Thus one wonders if the great bulk of human-kind can be truthfully called either cultured or civilized.) Here, in this repository of moral instruction, in its 31 chapters, 915 verses, approximately 900 proverbs, and 15,043 words, the journey that we call a life is presented as a canvas upon which the individual paints skillfully a civilized self-portrait – an offering – that will please himself and the Lord. In chapter 3, we are told, 'Happy is the man that findeth wisdom.' The Hebrew word for 'wisdom' is *chokmah*. It occurs no less than thirty-seven times in *Proverbs*. *Chokmah* also means skillfulness in dealing with the job that is before us – life itself – and I believe it is comparable to the Greek word *techne*, the rational application of principles aimed at making or doing something well. The reader who takes *Proverbs* to heart, who believes like the Greeks that 'the unexamined life is not worth living', is by nature a lover of wisdom: a philosopher. For that is precisely what the word 'philosophy' means (*philein*, to love – *sophia*, wisdom).

I'm aware those words – 'wisdom', 'civilized' and 'philosophy' – may sound musty and antique to modern (or post-modern) ears. As so many have said, ours is an Era of

Relativism, or situational ethics, perhaps even of nihilism, an historical period in which *Proverbs* will for some readers seem right-wing and patriarchal, oppressive and harsh, dogmatic and illiberal. Many will regard its contents as obsolete for the conditions we face at the eleventh hour of the twentieth century because, above all else, we moderns value individual freedom. Unfortunately, our passion for liberty is often misunderstood as license or, more accurately, as licentiousness. Personally, as a Buddhist, I was at first wary of writing about this book, though I was raised on its vision in a midwestern, African Methodist Episcopal church. But after going over *Proverbs* a half dozen times, after opening myself to its spiritual core, which complements nicely the world's other great religious traditions, I re-discovered the gems it has offered western humanity for centuries. I saw in its gnostic truths the reason why Professor C E M Joad once defined decadence as 'the loss of an object in life'. In fact, I realized that *Proverbs* not only speaks powerfully to our morally adrift era, but describes rather well my own often benighted, rebellious-on-principle generation (the Baby Boomers) when it says, 'There is a generation that curseth their father, and doth not bless their mother. There is a generation that are pure in their own eyes, and yet is not washed from their filthiness' (30:11-12).

Chilling.

Like all rich, multi-layered digests, *Proverbs* was not the work of a day. Nor is it the product of a single author, though King Solomon, that Ur-figure among ancient wise men, is credited with having contributed two of its oldest sections

(1:1 and 1:10). Several centuries after the death of Israel's king, the men of Hezekiah (700 BCE) added chapters 25 through 29 from Solomonic material. In short, the book was built layer upon layer, one tissue at a time, borrowing its synthesized instructions from many ancient sources, and did not achieve its finished form until the fourth or fifth century BCE. It favors, one might say, an old, old coin that has traversed continents, picking up something from each one as it was passed down through centuries – advice on social etiquette, philanthropy, how to choose a wife, and why children may need an occasional dose of Dr Spanker's tonic (the 'rod') – and bears the sweat and palm-oil of millions who have handled it. Bible scholar Kenneth T Aitken persuasively argues in his commentary *Proverbs* that the third section of the text (chapter 22) takes a few pages from the *Instructions of Amenemopet*.* That work, dating back to between 1000 and 600 BCE, was strictly a manual of professional training aimed at helping Egyptian civil servants achieve successful careers as they served the state. The sages of Israel, says Aitken, reworked some of the precepts from *Instructions* and at the same time re-contextualized them in a book far broader in its teachings for a triumphant life.

And these were, of course, originally *oral* teachings. They were delivered by a sage to pupils he addressed as a father would his children. His young charges were expected to memorize the proverbs until they were hard-wired into their

---

* Kenneth T Aitken, *Proverbs* (The Westminster Press: Philadelphia, 1968), p. 3.

hearts. Thus, this book was written for the ear. It relies heavily on repetition, a mnemonic device (which might weary modern eyes), and in its compositional strategies employs couplets linked by parallelisms. In his exegesis of *Proverbs*, J Vernon McGee identifies three forms of parallelisms that occur in the text: (1) *Synonymous Parallelism*, where the second clause restates the content of the first ('Judgments are prepared for scorners, and stripes for the back of the fool', 19:29). (2) *Antithetic (Contrast) Parallelism* that states a truth in the first clause, then contrasts it with an opposite truth in the second ('The light of the righteous rejoiceth, but the lamp of the wicked shall be put out', 13:9). And (3) *Synthetic Parallelism* in which the second clause develops the truth of the first ('The terror of a king is as the roaring of a lion; whoso provoketh him to anger sinneth against his own life', 20:2).*

Yet, for all the sophisticated architectonics in *Proverbs*, and for all the complexity of its literary pedigree, this is a book that sketches out a compelling, classic story: a pilgrim's progress. Imagine a young man (or woman) about to embark on life's journey. Call him – well, Pilgrim. Then, as now, the world teemed with a kaleidoscope of temptations, stramash and confusion. In the bustling cities where colorful bazaars, beggers, thieves, perfumed harlots, con-men, murderers, insouciant idlers and false teachers eager to entice a young person toward wrong-doing and sin (one hoary meaning of which is 'to miss the mark'), all can be found in great

---

* J Vernon McGee, *Proverbs* (Thomas Nelson Publishers: Nashville, 1991), p. x.

charles johnson

abundance. Indeed, these players, some as beautiful as Satan and who say, 'Let us lay wait for blood, let us lurk privily for the innocent', have from time immemorial taken advantage of callow youths (as well as given writers as diverse as Voltaire, De Sade, Dickens, Fielding and Maugham inexhaustible material for the *Bildungsroman*). Given a strictly materialistic viewpoint, it follows that the world of matter, mere *stuff*, will be dominated everywhere and in any era by those who treat objects and others as *things* to be used for their own pleasure and profit, and view everything through the lens of their own limited consciousness. Surveying this social field, we can imagine the authors of *Proverbs* agreeing with Thomas à Kempis who, in *The Imitation of Christ*, wearily quotes the Stoic philosopher Seneca, 'A wise man once said, "As often as I have been among men, I have returned home a lesser man"... No man can live in the public eye without risk to his soul ...'*

As we have seen, if our young Pilgrim is not to lose his (or her) soul on this planet where everything is provisional, if he is not to end bellied up and bottomed out, he needs a damned good map. Ethically, he should not have to reinvent the wheel each time he is confronted by a new moral dilemma. That, I believe, would be like a physicist claiming he can learn nothing from Galileo, Newton, Copernicus or Einstein because the conditions of their time differed so much from his own. But young people are notorious for for-

---

* Thomas à Kempis, *The Imitation of Christ*, trans. by Leo Sherley-Price (Penguin Books Ltd: Middlesex, 1953), p. 50.

getting instructions (ask any teacher about that), especially the 900 lessons on living delivered in *Proverbs*. What Pilgrim needs is the teaching condensed into *one* simple, bare-knuckled mantra that encapsulates the pith of all the other proverbs. Anticipating just this problem, the *Proverbs* authors provide that axiom in the very first chapter: 'The fear of the Lord is the beginning of knowledge: but fools despise wisdom and instruction.' From this one antithetic parallelism, this stern and admonishing couplet – moment by moment mindfulness of the Most High – all else in *Proverbs* follows with Mandarin exactitude and the necessity of a logical proof. Pilgrim is counseled to 'Commit thy works unto the Lord, and thy thoughts shall be established' (16:3), for the authors of this text understood the irrefragable fact that all we are is the result of what we have thought. From intellection comes desire. From desire, will. From will, our deeds. And from deeds, our destiny. Self-control, therefore, is so essential for the spiritual life and a practical life well led that it is even favorably compared to martial conquest: 'He that is slow to anger is better than the mighty; and he that ruleth his spirit than he that taketh a city' (16:32) in a line strikingly similar to one equally famous that we find in the first-century BCE Buddhist *Dhammapada* ('Path of Virtue') – 'If one man conquer in battle a thousand times a thousand men, and if another conquers himself, he is the greatest of conquerors.'* In the world's religious traditions, eastern and

---

* *The Dhammapada*, trans. by Irving Babbitt (New Directions: New York, 1965), p.18.

western, the Way of understanding and wisdom begins by sumptuously feeding the spirit and starving the illusory sense of the ego into extinction ('Trust in the Lord with all thine heart; and lean not unto thine own understanding. In all thy ways acknowledge him, and he shall direct thy paths. Be not wise in thine own eyes:' (3:5-7)), and is realized through a worldly practice that gives priority to the experience of our elders (our global inheritance) over ephemerae in a life that embodies humility, service, and a culture's loftiest ideals, which in Pilgrim's case would be the Ten Commandments.

Wisdom in *Proverbs*, we might say, is thought winging its way home.

Naturally, many couplets in *Proverbs* inveigh against people who are *not* mindful, those who 'eat the bread of wickedness and drink the wine of violence', and break the Commandments. This book does not suffer fools gladly. At first glance, Pilgrim might see the less demanding, hedonistic path and its players as alluring and sweet – and fun! But the seeds of *Proverbs* (practical wisdom) cannot grow in that polluted soil (the 'froward'). Pilgrim is advised not to envy or even 'fret' over the fallen state of these caitiffs and poltroons, for the Lord shall 'render to every man according to his works'. In other words, just as there is inexorable causation in the physical realm, so too is there cause-and-effect in the moral universe. The kingdom of God, at bottom, is a meritocracy; its logic is that of *karma* ('as you sow so shall you reap'). The unmindful cause their own downfall – they 'eat of the fruit of their own way'. Time and again,

Proverbs drives this point home, and nowhere more vividly than in its parable-like description of the industrious ant, or when the book cautions against lapses of vigilance in language so lovely the words almost pirouette and leap on the page: 'Yet a little sleep, a little slumber, a little folding of the hands to sleep: so shall thy poverty come as one that traveleth; and thy want as an armed man' (25:33-4).

However, it would be wrong to say that *Proverbs* is simply a map for avoiding life's pitfalls in order to bow one's knees to Baal. Throughout its chapters, Pilgrim is urged, 'Labor not to be rich' and he is reminded how 'riches certainly make themselves wings; they fly away as an eagle toward heaven', and 'Better is the poor that walketh in his uprightness, than he that is perverse in his ways, though he be rich'. Does this advice contradict the practicality that infuses *Proverbs*? Does it ask us to be poor? No, for a crucial distinction is drawn: 'Wealth gotten by vanity shall be diminished: but he that gathereth by labor shall increase'. The book points our Pilgrim toward industry, not that he might be 'greedy of gain', but rather that he or she might become the sort of provider who 'leaveth an inheritance to his children's children', honors his mother and father (and, one might add, his teachers), and 'stretcheth out her hand to the poor'. In effect, Pilgrim's labor is for others. Always life's true wealth in *Proverbs* is found in God, in wisdom and love; and love is realized through work and indefatigable service to the things loved.

In *Proverbs*, the portrait – the character sketch – that emerges of a successful pilgrim is that of a man or woman who is a quiet embodiment of culture. Not perfect by any means because he knows all too well his flaws. But in his life of building, serving, creating, he mightily strives to be righteous. He is soft-spoken and hates lying. In him there is the continuity of generations, one of the requisites for civilization itself. He is the joy of his mother and father and his children as well, for by honoring the wisdom of his predecessors and transmitting that (along with the fruit of his industry) to his posterity, his past (parents) meets his present (children) and vouchsafes their future. His good name the pilgrim values highly, and he is not garrulous, knowing how to hold his tongue and keep his own counsel. He never acts rashly or 'answereth a matter before he heareth it'. Concerning the needy, he is socially conscious and never 'stoppeth his ears at the cry of the poor'. Though he experiences failure and 'falleth seven times', the just man struggles to his feet again to do the Lord's work, ignoring his weariness. According to *Proverbs*, at night his sleep is 'sweet'. Such a person always heeds the helpful criticism of friends, but never wearies them with his presence or overstays his welcome. And, despite his hard-won victories and integrity, he never boasts, allowing instead 'another man [to] praise thee, and not thine own mouth'. Finally, the man of mindfulness is the very foundation of society – 'bold as a lion', the sort of citizen who, if he assumes a position of authority in the state, makes the 'people rejoice'.

Clearly, the path mapped out in *Proverbs* is exacting. Straight and narrow, 'like the edge of a sword', as Mahatma Gandhi once described the spiritual life. It is fitting, then, that *Proverbs* ends by letting our pilgrim know that he need not – indeed *can*not – travel to his goal alone. The righteous man needs a companion, a spouse equally mindful and just who will 'do him good and not evil all the days of her life'. A life-partner of such luminous morality that his heart 'doth safely trust in her, so that he shall have no need of spoil'. And so, in its remarkable finale – just before the curtain falls – this Old Testament book extolling wisdom and virtue closes by incarnating its heady idealism in an astonishing homage to the *concrete* beauty and goodness of God-fearing women (one surely influential for Chaucer's Wife of Bath), a breathtaking, unforgettable praise-song to this 'good thing', this 'favor of the Lord', this ravishing 'wife of thy youth':

> Strength and honor are her clothing;
> > and she shall rejoice in time to come.
> She openeth her mouth with wisdom;
> > and in her tongue is the law of kindness.
> She looketh well to the ways of her household,
> > and eateth not the bread of idleness.
> Her children arise up and call her blessed;
> > her husband also, and he praiseth her.

May we all be blessed with such radiant partners. And, as we travel through this life, may we recognize that *Proverbs*, in its fierce, uncompromising purity, is a work worthy of our trust.

the proverbs

The proverbs of Solomon the son of David, king of Israel:

²to know wisdom and instruction;
   to perceive the words of understanding;
³to receive the instruction of wisdom, justice,
   and judgment, and equity;
⁴to give subtilty to the simple,
   to the young man knowledge and discretion.
⁵A wise man will hear, and will increase learning;
   and a man of understanding
      shall attain unto wise counsels:
⁶to understand a proverb, and the interpretation;
   the words of the wise, and their dark sayings.

⁷The fear of the Lord is the beginning of knowledge:
   but fools despise wisdom and instruction.
⁸My son, hear the instruction of thy father,
   and forsake not the law of thy mother,
⁹for they shall be an ornament of grace unto thy head,
   and chains about thy neck.

¹⁰My son, if sinners entice thee, consent thou not.

¹¹ If they say, 'Come with us, let us lay wait for blood,
  let us lurk privily for the innocent without cause':
¹² Let us swallow them up alive as the grave;
  and whole, as those that go down into the pit:
¹³ We shall find all precious substance,
  we shall fill our houses with spoil.
¹⁴ Cast in thy lot among us;
  let us all have one purse:
¹⁵ My son, walk not thou in the way with them;
  refrain thy foot from their path:
¹⁶ For their feet run to evil,
  and make haste to shed blood.
¹⁷ Surely in vain the net is spread
  in the sight of any bird.
¹⁸ And they lay wait for their own blood;
  they lurk privily for their own lives.
¹⁹ So are the ways of every one that is greedy of gain,
  which taketh away the life of the owners thereof.

²⁰ Wisdom crieth without;
  she uttereth her voice in the streets.
²¹ She crieth in the chief place of concourse,
  in the openings of the gates:
      in the city she uttereth her words, saying,
²² 'How long, ye simple ones, will ye love simplicity?'
  And the scorners delight in their scorning,
      and fools hate knowledge?

23 Turn you at my reproof;
 behold, I will pour out my spirit unto you,
  I will make known my words unto you.

24 'Because I have called, and ye refused;
 I have stretched out my hand,
  and no man regarded;
25 but ye have set at nought all my counsel,
 and would none of my reproof.
26 I also will laugh at your calamity;
 I will mock when your fear cometh;
27 when your fear cometh as desolation,
 and your destruction cometh as a whirlwind;
  when distress and anguish cometh upon you.
28 Then shall they call upon me, but I will not answer;
 they shall seek me early,
  but they shall not find me:
29 for that they hated knowledge,
 and did not choose the fear of the Lord.
30 They would none of my counsel;
 they despised all my reproof.
31 Therefore shall they eat of the fruit of their own way,
 and be filled with their own devices.
32 For the turning away of the simple shall slay them,
 and the prosperity of fools shall destroy them.
33 But whoso hearkeneth unto me shall dwell safely,
 and shall be quiet from fear of evil.

2 My son, if thou wilt receive my words,
and hide my commandments with thee;
[2] so that thou incline thine ear unto wisdom,
and apply thine heart to understanding;
[3] yea, if thou criest after knowledge,
and liftest up thy voice for understanding,
[4] if thou seekest her as silver,
and searchest for her as for hid treasures:
[5] then shalt thou understand the fear of the Lord,
and find the knowledge of God.
[6] For the Lord giveth wisdom:
out of his mouth cometh knowledge
and understanding.
[7] He layeth up sound wisdom for the righteous;
he is a buckler to them that walk uprightly.
[8] He keepeth the paths of judgment,
and preserveth the way of his saints.
[9] Then shalt thou understand righteousness,
and judgment, and equity;
yea, every good path.

[10] When wisdom entereth into thine heart,
and knowledge is pleasant unto thy soul;
[11] discretion shall preserve thee,
understanding shall keep thee:
[12] To deliver thee from the way of the evil man,
from the man that speaketh froward things;

¹³ who leave the paths of uprightness,
     to walk in the ways of darkness;
¹⁴ who rejoice to do evil,
     and delight in the frowardness of the wicked;
¹⁵ whose ways are crooked,
     and they froward in their paths:
¹⁶ to deliver thee from the strange woman,
     even from the stranger
        which flattereth with her words;
¹⁷ which forsaketh the guide of her youth,
     and forgetteth the covenant of her God.
¹⁸ For her house inclineth unto death,
     and her paths unto the dead.
¹⁹ None that go unto her return again,
     neither take they hold of the paths of life.
²⁰ That thou mayest walk in the way of good men,
     and keep the paths of the righteous.
²¹ For the upright shall dwell in the land,
     and the perfect shall remain in it.
²² But the wicked shall be cut off from the earth,
     and the transgressors shall be rooted out of it.

3 My son, forget not my law;
     but let thine heart keep my commandments:
² For length of days, and long life,
     and peace, shall they add to thee.

³ Let not mercy and truth forsake thee:
    bind them about thy neck;
        write them upon the table of thine heart:
⁴ so shalt thou find favour and good understanding
    in the sight of God and man.

⁵ Trust in the Lord with all thine heart;
    and lean not unto thine own understanding.
⁶ In all thy ways acknowledge him,
    and he shall direct thy paths.

⁷ Be not wise in thine own eyes:
    fear the Lord, and depart from evil.
⁸ It shall be health to thy navel,
    and marrow to thy bones.
⁹ Honour the Lord with thy substance,
    and with the first-fruits of all thine increase:
¹⁰ so shall thy barns be filled with plenty,
    and thy presses shall burst out with new wine.

¹¹ My son, despise not the chastening of the Lord;
    neither be weary of his correction:
¹² for whom the Lord loveth he correcteth;
    even as a father the son in whom he delighteth.

¹³ Happy is the man that findeth wisdom,
    and the man that getteth understanding.

[14] For the merchandise of it is better
than the merchandise of silver,
and the gain thereof than fine gold.
[15] She is more precious than rubies:
and all the things thou canst desire
are not to be compared unto her.
[16] Length of days is in her right hand;
and in her left hand riches and honour.
[17] Her ways are ways of pleasantness,
and all her paths are peace.
[18] She is a tree of life to them that lay hold upon her:
and happy is every one that retaineth her.
[19] The Lord by wisdom hath founded the earth;
by understanding hath he established the heavens.
[20] By his knowledge the depths are broken up,
and the clouds drop down the dew.
[21] My son, let not them depart from thine eyes:
keep sound wisdom and discretion:
[22] so shall they be life unto thy soul,
and grace to thy neck.
[23] Then shalt thou walk in thy way safely,
and thy foot shall not stumble.
[24] When thou liest down, thou shalt not be afraid:
yea, thou shalt lie down,
and thy sleep shall be sweet.

²⁵ Be not afraid of sudden fear,
   neither of the desolation of the wicked,
      when it cometh.
²⁶ For the Lord shall be thy confidence,
   and shall keep thy foot from being taken.

²⁷ Withhold not good from them to whom it is due,
   when it is in the power of thine hand to do it.
²⁸ Say not unto thy neighbour,
   'Go, and come again, and tomorrow I will give,'
      when thou hast it by thee.
²⁹ Devise not evil against thy neighbour,
   seeing he dwelleth securely by thee.

³⁰ Strive not with a man without cause,
   if he have done thee no harm.

³¹ Envy thou not the oppressor,
   and choose none of his ways.
³² For the froward is abomination to the Lord:
   but his secret is with the righteous.

³³ The curse of the Lord is in the house of the wicked:
   but he blesseth the habitation of the just.
³⁴ Surely he scorneth the scorners:
   but he giveth grace unto the lowly.
³⁵ The wise shall inherit glory:
   but shame shall be the promotion of fools.

4 Hear, ye children, the instruction of a father,
and attend to know understanding.
² For I give you good doctrine,
forsake ye not my law.
³ For I was my father's son,
tender and only beloved in the sight of my mother.
⁴ He taught me also, and said unto me,
'Let thine heart retain my words:
keep my commandments, and live.
⁵ Get wisdom, get understanding:
forget it not;
neither decline from the words of my mouth.
⁶ Forsake her not, and she shall preserve thee:
love her, and she shall keep thee.
⁷ Wisdom is the principal thing;
therefore get wisdom:
and with all thy getting get understanding.
⁸ Exalt her, and she shall promote thee:
she shall bring thee to honour,
when thou dost embrace her.
⁹ She shall give to thine head an ornament of grace:
a crown of glory shall she deliver to thee.'
¹⁰ Hear, O my son, and receive my sayings;
and the years of thy life shall be many.
¹¹ I have taught thee in the way of wisdom;
I have led thee in right paths.

¹² When thou goest, thy steps shall not be straitened;
  and when thou runnest, thou shalt not stumble.
¹³ Take fast hold of instruction;
  let her not go: keep her; for she is thy life.

¹⁴ Enter not into the path of the wicked,
  and go not in the way of evil men.
¹⁵ Avoid it, pass not by it,
  turn from it, and pass away.
¹⁶ For they sleep not, except they have done mischief;
  and their sleep is taken away,
    unless they cause some to fall.
¹⁷ For they eat the bread of wickedness,
  and drink the wine of violence.
¹⁸ But the path of the just is as the shining light,
  that shineth more and more unto the perfect day.
¹⁹ The way of the wicked is as darkness:
  they know not at what they stumble.

²⁰ My son, attend to my words;
  incline thine ear unto my sayings.
²¹ Let them not depart from thine eyes;
  keep them in the midst of thine heart.
²² For they are life unto those that find them,
  and health to all their flesh.

²³ Keep thy heart with all diligence;
  for out of it are the issues of life.

²⁴ Put away from thee a froward mouth,
and perverse lips put far from thee.
²⁵ Let thine eyes look right on,
and let thine eyelids
look straight before thee.
²⁶ Ponder the path of thy feet,
and let all thy ways be established.
²⁷ Turn not to the right hand nor to the left:
remove thy foot from evil.

5 My son, attend unto my wisdom,
and bow thine ear to my understanding:
² that thou mayest regard discretion,
and that thy lips may keep knowledge.

³ For the lips of a strange woman
drop as an honeycomb,
and her mouth is smoother than oil:
⁴ But her end is bitter as wormwood,
sharp as a two-edged sword.
⁵ Her feet go down to death;
her steps take hold on hell.
⁶ Lest thou shouldest ponder the path of life,
her ways are moveable,
that thou canst not know them.
⁷ Hear me now therefore, O ye children,
and depart not from the words of my mouth.

⁸ Remove thy way far from her,
    and come not nigh the door of her house:
⁹ Lest thou give thine honour unto others,
    and thy years unto the cruel:
¹⁰ lest strangers be filled with thy wealth;
    and thy labours be in the house of a stranger;
¹¹ and thou mourn at the last,
    when thy flesh and thy body are consumed,
¹² and say, 'How have I hated instruction,
    and my heart despised reproof;
¹³ and have not obeyed the voice of my teachers,
    nor inclined mine ear
        to them that instructed me!'
¹⁴ I was almost in all evil
    in the midst of the congregation and assembly.

¹⁵ Drink waters out of thine own cistern,
    and running waters out of thine own well.
¹⁶ Let thy fountains be dispersed abroad,
    and rivers of waters in the streets.
¹⁷ Let them be only thine own,
    and not strangers with thee.
¹⁸ Let thy fountain be blessed:
    and rejoice with the wife of thy youth.
¹⁹ Let her be as the loving hind and pleasant roe;
    let her breasts satisfy thee at all times;
        and be thou ravished
    always with her love.

²⁰And why wilt thou, my son,
    be ravished with a strange woman,
        and embrace the bosom of a stranger?
²¹For the ways of man are before the eyes of the Lord,
    and he pondereth all his goings.
²²His own iniquities shall take the wicked himself,
    and he shall be holden with the cords of his sins.
²³He shall die without instruction;
    and in the greatness of his folly
        he shall go astray.

6

My son, if thou be surety for thy friend,
    if thou hast stricken thy hand with a stranger,
²thou art snared with the words of thy mouth,
    thou art taken with the words of thy mouth.
³Do this now, my son, and deliver thyself,
    when thou art come into the hand of thy friend;
        go, humble thyself, and make sure thy friend.
⁴Give not sleep to thine eyes,
    nor slumber to thine eyelids.
⁵Deliver thyself as a roe from the hand of the hunter,
    and as a bird from the hand of the fowler.

⁶Go to the ant, thou sluggard;
    consider her ways, and be wise:
⁷which having no guide, overseer, or ruler,
⁸provideth her meat in the summer,
    and gathereth her food in the harvest.

⁹ How long wilt thou sleep, O sluggard?
  When wilt thou arise out of thy sleep?
¹⁰ Yet a little sleep, a little slumber,
  a little folding of the hands to sleep:
¹¹ so shall thy poverty come as one that travaileth,
  and thy want as an armed man.

¹² A naughty person, a wicked man,
  walketh with a froward mouth.
¹³ He winketh with his eyes,
  he speaketh with his feet,
    he teacheth with his fingers;
¹⁴ frowardness is in his heart,
  he deviseth mischief continually;
    he soweth discord.
¹⁵ Therefore shall his calamity come suddenly;
  suddenly shall he be broken without remedy.

¹⁶ These six things doth the Lord hate;
  yea, seven are an abomination unto him:
¹⁷ a proud look, a lying tongue,
  and hands that shed innocent blood,
¹⁸ an heart that deviseth wicked imaginations,
  feet that be swift in running to mischief,
¹⁹ a false witness that speaketh lies,
  and he that soweth discord among brethren.

²⁰ My son, keep thy father's commandment,
  and forsake not the law of thy mother:

²¹ bind them continually upon thine heart,
and tie them about thy neck.
²² When thou goest, it shall lead thee;
when thou sleepest, it shall keep thee;
and when thou awakest,
it shall talk with thee.
²³ For the commandment is a lamp;
and the law is light;
and reproofs of instruction are the way of life:
²⁴ To keep thee from the evil woman,
from the flattery
of the tongue of a strange woman.
²⁵ Lust not after her beauty in thine heart;
neither let her take thee with her eyelids.
²⁶ For by means of a whorish woman
a man is brought to a piece of bread:
and the adulteress will hunt for
the precious life.
²⁷ Can a man take fire in his bosom,
and his clothes not be burned?
²⁸ Can one go upon hot coals,
and his feet not be burned?
²⁹ So he that goeth in to his neighbour's wife;
whosoever toucheth her shall not be innocent.
³⁰ Men do not despise a thief,
if he steal to satisfy his soul when he is hungry;
³¹ but if he be found, he shall restore sevenfold;
he shall give all the substance of his house.

³² But whoso committeth adultery with a woman
lacketh understanding:
he that doeth it destroyeth his own soul.
³³ A wound and dishonour shall he get;
and his reproach shall not be wiped away.
³⁴ For jealousy is the rage of a man:
therefore he will not spare
in the day of vengeance.
³⁵ He will not regard any ransom;
neither will he rest content,
though thou givest many gifts.

7   My son, keep my words,
and lay up my commandments with thee.
² Keep my commandments, and live;
and my law as the apple of thine eye.
³ Bind them upon thy fingers,
write them upon the table of thine heart.
⁴ Say unto wisdom, 'Thou art my sister,'
and call understanding thy kinswoman:
⁵ that they may keep thee
from the strange woman,
from the stranger
which flattereth
with her words.
⁶ For at the window of my house
I looked through my casement,

⁷and beheld among the simple ones,
  I discerned among the youths,
      a young man void of understanding,
⁸ passing through the street near her corner;
  and he went the way to her house,
⁹ in the twilight, in the evening,
  in the black and dark night:
¹⁰And, behold, there met him a woman
  with the attire of an harlot, and subtil of heart.
¹¹(She is loud and stubborn;
  her feet abide not in her house:
¹² now is she without, now in the streets,
  and lieth in wait at every corner.)
¹³ So she caught him, and kissed him,
  and with an impudent face said unto him,
¹⁴ 'I have peace offerings with me;
  this day have I payed my vows.
¹⁵ Therefore came I forth to meet thee,
  diligently to seek thy face, and I have found thee.
¹⁶ I have decked my bed with coverings of tapestry,
  with carved works, with fine linen of Egypt.
¹⁷ I have perfumed my bed with myrrh,
  aloes, and cinnamon.
¹⁸ Come, let us take our fill of love until the morning;
  let us solace ourselves with loves.
¹⁹ For the goodman is not at home,
  he is gone a long journey:

²⁰ he hath taken a bag of money with him,
and will come home at the day appointed.'
²¹ With her much fair speech she caused him to yield,
with the flattering of her lips she forced him.
²² He goeth after her straightway,
as an ox goeth to the slaughter,
or as a fool to the correction of the stocks;
²³ till a dart strike through his liver;
as a bird hasteth to the snare,
and knoweth not that it is for his life.

²⁴ Hearken unto me now therefore, O ye children,
and attend to the words of my mouth.
²⁵ Let not thine heart decline to her ways,
go not astray in her paths.
²⁶ For she hath cast down many wounded;
yea, many strong men have been slain by her.
²⁷ Her house is the way to hell,
going down to the chambers of death.

8   Doth not wisdom cry?
And understanding put forth her voice?
² She standeth in the top of high places,
by the way in the places of the paths.
³ She crieth at the gates, at the entry of the city,
at the coming in at the doors,
⁴ 'Unto you, O men, I call;

and my voice is to the sons of man.
⁵ O ye simple, understand wisdom, and, ye fools,
    be ye of an understanding heart.
⁶ Hear; for I will speak of excellent things;
    and the opening of my lips shall be right things.
⁷ For my mouth shall speak truth;
    and wickedness is an abomination to my lips.
⁸ All the words of my mouth are in righteousness;
    there is nothing froward or perverse in them.
⁹ They are all plain to him that understandeth,
    and right to them that find knowledge.
¹⁰ Receive my instruction, and not silver;
    and knowledge rather than choice gold.
¹¹ For wisdom is better than rubies;
    and all the things that may be desired
        are not to be compared to it.

¹² I wisdom dwell with prudence,
    and find out knowledge of witty inventions.
¹³ The fear of the Lord is to hate evil;
    pride, and arrogancy, and the evil way,
        and the froward mouth, do I hate.
¹⁴ Counsel is mine, and sound wisdom.
    I am understanding; I have strength.
¹⁵ By me kings reign, and princes decree justice.
¹⁶ By me princes rule, and nobles,
    even all the judges of the earth.

¹⁷ I love them that love me;
   and those that seek me early shall find me.
¹⁸ Riches and honour are with me;
   yea, durable riches and righteousness.
¹⁹ My fruit is better than gold, yea, than fine gold;
   and my revenue than choice silver.
²⁰ I lead in the way of righteousness,
   in the midst of the paths of judgment:
²¹ that I may cause those that love me
      to inherit substance;
         and I will fill their treasures.

²² The Lord possessed me in the beginning of his way,
   before his works of old.
²³ I was set up from everlasting,
   from the beginning, or ever the earth was.
²⁴ When there were no depths, I was brought forth;
   when there were no fountains
      abounding with water.
²⁵ Before the mountains were settled,
   before the hills was I brought forth:
²⁶ while as yet he had not made the earth, nor the fields,
   nor the highest part of the dust of the world.
²⁷ When he prepared the heavens, I was there:
   when he set a compass upon the face of the depth:
²⁸ when he established the clouds above:
   when he strengthened the fountains of the deep:

²⁹ when he gave to the sea his decree,
    that the waters should not
        pass his commandment:
    when he appointed the foundations of the earth:
³⁰ then I was by him, as one brought up with him:
    and I was daily his delight,
        rejoicing always before him;
³¹ rejoicing in the habitable part of his earth;
    and my delights were with the sons of men.

³² Now therefore hearken unto me, O ye children:
    for blessed are they that keep my ways.
³³ Hear instruction, and be wise, and refuse it not.
³⁴ Blessed is the man that heareth me,
    watching daily at my gates,
        waiting at the posts of my doors.
³⁵ For whoso findeth me findeth life,
    and shall obtain favour of the Lord.
³⁶ But he that sinneth against me
    wrongeth his own soul:
        all they that hate me love death.'

9 Wisdom hath builded her house,
    she hath hewn out her seven pillars.
² She hath killed her beasts;
    she hath mingled her wine;
        she hath also furnished her table.

³ She hath sent forth her maidens:
  she crieth upon the highest places of the city,
⁴ 'Whoso is simple, let him turn in hither.'
  As for him that wanteth understanding,
    she saith to him,
⁵ 'Come, eat of my bread, and drink of the wine
  which I have mingled.
⁶ Forsake the foolish, and live;
  and go in the way of understanding.'
⁷ He that reproveth a scorner getteth to himself shame:
  and he that rebuketh a wicked man
    getteth himself a blot.
⁸ Reprove not a scorner, lest he hate thee:
  rebuke a wise man, and he will love thee.
⁹ Give instruction to a wise man,
  and he will be yet wiser:
    teach a just man,
  and he will increase in learning.

¹⁰ The fear of the Lord is the beginning of wisdom:
  and the knowledge of the holy is understanding.
¹¹ For by me thy days shall be multiplied,
  and the years of thy life shall be increased.
¹² If thou be wise, thou shalt be wise for thyself:
  but if thou scornest, thou alone shalt bear it.

¹³ A foolish woman is clamorous:
  she is simple, and knoweth nothing.

¹⁴ For she sitteth at the door of her house,
    on a seat in the high places of the city,
¹⁵ to call passengers who go right on their ways:
¹⁶ 'Whoso is simple, let him turn in hither,'
    and as for him that wanteth understanding,
        she saith to him,
¹⁷ 'Stolen waters are sweet,
    and bread eaten in secret is pleasant.'
¹⁸ But he knoweth not that the dead are there;
    and that her guests are in the depths of hell.

10 The proverbs of Solomon.

A wise son maketh a glad father:
    but a foolish son is the heaviness of his mother.

² Treasures of wickedness profit nothing:
    but righteousness delivereth from death.

³ The Lord will not suffer
    the soul of the righteous to famish:
        but he casteth away
    the substance of the wicked.

⁴ He becometh poor that dealeth with a slack hand:
    but the hand of the diligent maketh rich.

⁵ He that gathereth in summer is a wise son:
    but he that sleepeth in harvest
        is a son that causeth shame.

[6] Blessings are upon the head of the just:
  but violence covereth the mouth of the wicked.

[7] The memory of the just is blessed:
  but the name of the wicked shall rot.

[8] The wise in heart will receive commandments:
  but a prating fool shall fall.

[9] He that walketh uprightly walketh surely:
  but he that perverteth his ways shall be known.

[10] He that winketh with the eye causeth sorrow:
  but a prating fool shall fall.

[11] The mouth of a righteous man is a well of life:
  but violence covereth the mouth of the wicked.

[12] Hatred stirreth up strifes:
  but love covereth all sins.

[13] In the lips of him that hath understanding
  wisdom is found:
      but a rod is for the back of him
    that is void of understanding.

[14] Wise men lay up knowledge:
  but the mouth of the foolish
      is near destruction.

[15] The rich man's wealth is his strong city:
  the destruction of the poor is their poverty.

¹⁶ The labour of the righteous tendeth to life:
the fruit of the wicked to sin.

¹⁷ He is in the way of life that keepeth instruction:
but he that refuseth reproof erreth.

¹⁸ He that hideth hatred with lying lips,
and he that uttereth a slander, is a fool.

¹⁹ In the multitude of words there wanteth not sin:
but he that refraineth his lips is wise.

²⁰ The tongue of the just is as choice silver:
the heart of the wicked is little worth.

²¹ The lips of the righteous feed many:
but fools die for want of wisdom.

²² The blessing of the Lord, it maketh rich,
and he addeth no sorrow with it.

²³ It is as sport to a fool to do mischief:
but a man of understanding hath wisdom:

²⁴ The fear of the wicked, it shall come upon him:
but the desire of the righteous shall be granted.

²⁵ As the whirlwind passeth, so is the wicked no more:
but the righteous is an everlasting foundation.

²⁶ As vinegar to the teeth, and as smoke to the eyes,
so is the sluggard to them that send him.

²⁷ The fear of the Lord prolongeth days:
    but the years of the wicked shall be shortened.

²⁸ The hope of the righteous shall be gladness:
    but the expectation of the wicked shall perish.

²⁹ The way of the Lord is strength to the upright:
    but destruction shall be to the workers of iniquity.

³⁰ The righteous shall never be removed:
    but the wicked shall not inhabit the earth.

³¹ The mouth of the just bringeth forth wisdom:
    but the froward tongue shall be cut out.

³² The lips of the righteous know what is acceptable:
    but the mouth of the wicked speaketh frowardness.

11 A false balance is abomination to the Lord:
    but a just weight is his delight.

² When pride cometh, then cometh shame:
    but with the lowly is wisdom.

³ The integrity of the upright shall guide them:
    but the perverseness of transgressors
        shall destroy them.

⁴ Riches profit not in the day of wrath:
    but righteousness delivereth from death.

⁵ The righteousness of the perfect
   shall direct his way:
      but the wicked
   shall fall by his own wickedness.

⁶ The righteousness of the upright shall deliver them:
   but transgressors shall be taken
      in their own naughtiness.

⁷ When a wicked man dieth,
   his expectation shall perish:
      and the hope of unjust men perisheth.

⁸ The righteous is delivered out of trouble,
   and the wicked cometh in his stead.

⁹ An hypocrite with his mouth
   destroyeth his neighbour:
      but through knowledge
   shall the just be delivered.

¹⁰ When it goeth well with the righteous,
   the city rejoiceth:
      and when the wicked perish, there is shouting.

¹¹ By the blessing of the upright the city is exalted:
   but it is overthrown by the mouth of the wicked.

¹² He that is void of wisdom despiseth his neighbour:
   but a man of understanding holdeth his peace.

¹³A talebearer revealeth secrets:
   but he that is of a faithful spirit
      concealeth the matter.

¹⁴Where no counsel is, the people fall:
   but in the multitude of counsellors there is safety.

¹⁵He that is surety for a stranger shall smart for it:
   and he that hateth suretiship is sure.

¹⁶A gracious woman retaineth honour:
   and strong men retain riches.

¹⁷The merciful man doeth good to his own soul:
   but he that is cruel troubleth his own flesh.

¹⁸The wicked worketh a deceitful work:
   but to him that soweth righteousness
      shall be a sure reward.

¹⁹As righteousness tendeth to life:
   so he that pursueth evil pursueth it
      to his own death.

²⁰They that are of a froward heart
      are abomination to the Lord:
   but such as are upright in their way
      are his delight.

²¹Though hand join in hand,
   the wicked shall not be unpunished:
      but the seed of the righteous shall be delivered.

²²As a jewel of gold in a swine's snout,
    so is a fair woman which is without discretion.

²³ The desire of the righteous is only good:
    but the expectation of the wicked is wrath.

²⁴ There is that scattereth, and yet increaseth;
    and there is that withholdeth more than is meet,
        but it tendeth to poverty.

²⁵ The liberal soul shall be made fat:
    and he that watereth shall be watered also himself.

²⁶ He that withholdeth corn, the people shall curse him:
    but blessing shall be upon the head of him
        that selleth it.

²⁷ He that diligently seeketh good procureth favour,
    but he that seeketh mischief,
        it shall come unto him.

²⁸ He that trusteth in his riches shall fall,
        but the righteous shall flourish as a branch.

²⁹ He that troubleth his own house
    shall inherit the wind:
        and the fool shall be servant
    to the wise of heart.

³⁰ The fruit of the righteous is a tree of life;
    and he that winneth souls is wise.

³¹ Behold, the righteous shall be recompensed
in the earth:
much more the wicked and the sinner.

12 Whoso loveth instruction loveth knowledge:
but he that hateth reproof is brutish.

²A good man obtaineth favour of the Lord:
but a man of wicked devices will he condemn.

³A man shall not be established by wickedness:
but the root of the righteous shall not be moved.

⁴A virtuous woman is a crown to her husband:
but she that maketh ashamed
is as rottenness in his bones.

⁵ The thoughts of the righteous are right:
but the counsels of the wicked are deceit.

⁶ The words of the wicked
are to lie in wait for blood:
but the mouth of the upright
shall deliver them.

⁷ The wicked are overthrown, and are not:
but the house of the righteous shall stand.

⁸A man shall be commended according to his wisdom:
but he that is of a perverse heart shall be despised.

⁹ He that is despised, and hath a servant,
   is better than he that honoureth himself,
      and lacketh bread.

¹⁰A righteous man regardeth the life of his beast,
   but the tender mercies of the wicked are cruel.

¹¹ He that tilleth his land shall be satisfied with bread:
   but he that followeth vain persons
      is void of understanding.

¹² The wicked desireth the net of evil men:
   but the root of the righteous yieldeth fruit.

¹³ The wicked is snared by the transgression of his lips:
   but the just shall come out of trouble.

¹⁴A man shall be satisfied with good
   by the fruit of his mouth,
      and the recompence of a man's hands
   shall be rendered unto him.

¹⁵ The way of a fool is right in his own eyes:
   but he that hearkeneth unto counsel is wise.

¹⁶A fool's wrath is presently known:
   but a prudent man covereth shame.

¹⁷ He that speaketh truth sheweth forth righteousness:
   but a false witness deceit.

¹⁸ There is that speaketh like the piercings of a sword:
   but the tongue of the wise is health.

¹⁹ The lip of truth shall be established for ever:
   but a lying tongue is but for a moment.

²⁰ Deceit is in the heart of them that imagine evil:
   but to the counsellors of peace is joy.

²¹ There shall no evil happen to the just:
   but the wicked shall be filled with mischief.

²² Lying lips are abomination to the Lord:
   but they that deal truly are his delight.

²³ A prudent man concealeth knowledge:
   but the heart of fools proclaimeth foolishness.

²⁴ The hand of the diligent shall bear rule:
   but the slothful shall be under tribute.

²⁵ Heaviness in the heart of man maketh it stoop:
   but a good word maketh it glad.

²⁶ The righteous is more excellent than his neighbour:
   but the way of the wicked seduceth them.

²⁷ The slothful man roasteth
   not that which he took in hunting:
      but the substance of a diligent man is precious.

²⁸ In the way of righteousness is life;
   and in the pathway thereof there is no death.

13

A wise son heareth his father's instruction:
    but a scorner heareth not rebuke.

2 A man shall eat good by the fruit of his mouth:
    but the soul of the transgressors
        shall eat violence.

3 He that keepeth his mouth keepeth his life:
    but he that openeth wide his lips
        shall have destruction.

4 The soul of the sluggard desireth, and hath nothing:
    but the soul of the diligent shall be made fat.

5 A righteous man hateth lying:
    but a wicked man is loathsome,
        and cometh to shame.

6 Righteousness keepeth him
    that is upright in the way:
        but wickedness overthroweth the sinner.

7 There is that maketh himself rich,
    yet hath nothing:
        there is that maketh himself poor,
    yet hath great riches.

8 The ransom of a man's life are his riches:
    but the poor heareth not rebuke.

9 The light of the righteous rejoiceth:
    but the lamp of the wicked shall be put out.

¹⁰ Only by pride cometh contention:
    but with the well advised is wisdom.

¹¹ Wealth gotten by vanity shall be diminished:
    but he that gathereth by labour shall increase.

¹² Hope deferred maketh the heart sick:
    but when the desire cometh, it is a tree of life.

¹³ Whoso despiseth the word shall be destroyed:
    but he that feareth the commandment
        shall be rewarded.

¹⁴ The law of the wise is a fountain of life,
    to depart from the snares of death.

¹⁵ Good understanding giveth favour:
    but the way of transgressors is hard.

¹⁶ Every prudent man dealeth with knowledge:
    but a fool layeth open his folly.

¹⁷ A wicked messenger falleth into mischief:
    but a faithful ambassador is health.

¹⁸ Poverty and shame shall be
    to him that refuseth instruction:
        but he that regardeth reproof
    shall be honoured.

¹⁹ The desire accomplished is sweet to the soul:
    but it is abomination to fools to depart from evil.

²⁰ He that walketh with wise men shall be wise:
   but a companion of fools shall be destroyed.

²¹ Evil pursueth sinners:
   but to the righteous good shall be repayed.

²² A good man leaveth an inheritance
   to his children's children:
         and the wealth of the sinner
   is laid up for the just.

²³ Much food is in the tillage of the poor:
   but there is that is destroyed
         for want of judgment.

²⁴ He that spareth his rod hateth his son:
   but he that loveth him chasteneth him betimes.

²⁵ The righteous eateth to the satisfying of his soul:
   but the belly of the wicked shall want.

14

Every wise woman buildeth her house:
   but the foolish plucketh it down with her hands.

² He that walketh in his uprightness
   feareth the Lord:
         but he that is perverse in his ways
   despiseth him.

³ In the mouth of the foolish is a rod of pride:
   but the lips of the wise shall preserve them.

⁴ Where no oxen are, the crib is clean:
　　but much increase is by the strength of the ox.

⁵ A faithful witness will not lie:
　　but a false witness will utter lies.

⁶ A scorner seeketh wisdom, and findeth it not:
　　but knowledge is easy unto him
　　　　that understandeth.

⁷ Go from the presence of a foolish man,
　　when thou perceivest not in him
　　　　the lips of knowledge.

⁸ The wisdom of the prudent
　　is to understand his way:
　　　　but the folly of fools is deceit.

⁹ Fools make a mock at sin:
　　but among the righteous there is favour.

¹⁰ The heart knoweth his own bitterness;
　　and a stranger doth not intermeddle with his joy.

¹¹ The house of the wicked shall be overthrown:
　　but the tabernacle of the upright shall flourish.

¹² There is a way which seemeth right unto a man,
　　but the end thereof are the ways of death.

¹³ Even in laughter the heart is sorrowful;
　　and the end of that mirth is heaviness.

¹⁴ The backslider in heart shall be filled
    with his own ways:
        and a good man shall be satisfied
    from himself.

¹⁵ The simple believeth every word:
    but the prudent man looketh well to his going.

¹⁶ A wise man feareth, and departeth from evil:
    but the fool rageth, and is confident.

¹⁷ He that is soon angry dealeth foolishly:
    and a man of wicked devices is hated.

¹⁸ The simple inherit folly:
    but the prudent are crowned with knowledge.

¹⁹ The evil bow before the good;
    and the wicked at the gates of the righteous.

²⁰ The poor is hated even of his own neighbour:
    but the rich hath many friends.

²¹ He that despiseth his neighbour sinneth:
    but he that hath mercy on the poor, happy is he.

²² Do they not err that devise evil?
    But mercy and truth shall be to them
        that devise good.

²³ In all labour there is profit:
    but the talk of the lips tendeth only to penury.

²⁴ The crown of the wise is their riches:
    but the foolishness of fools is folly.

²⁵ A true witness delivereth souls:
    but a deceitful witness
        speaketh lies.

²⁶ In the fear of the Lord is strong confidence:
    and his children shall have a place of refuge.

²⁷ The fear of the Lord is a fountain of life,
    to depart from the snares of death.

²⁸ In the multitude of people is the king's honour:
    but in the want of people
        is the destruction of the prince.

²⁹ He that is slow to wrath
    is of great understanding:
        but he that is hasty of spirit
    exalteth folly.

³⁰ A sound heart is the life of the flesh:
    but envy the rottenness of the bones.

³¹ He that oppresseth the poor
    reproacheth his Maker:
        but he that honoureth him
    hath mercy on the poor.

³² The wicked is driven away in his wickedness:
    but the righteous hath hope in his death.

³³ Wisdom resteth in the heart of him
    that hath understanding:
      but that which is in the midst of fools
    is made known.

³⁴ Righteousness exalteth a nation:
    but sin is a reproach to any people.

³⁵ The king's favour is toward a wise servant:
    but his wrath is against him that causeth shame.

15

A soft answer turneth away wrath:
    but grievous words stir up anger.

² The tongue of the wise useth knowledge aright:
    but the mouth of fools poureth out foolishness.

³ The eyes of the Lord are in every place,
    beholding the evil and the good.

⁴ A wholesome tongue is a tree of life:
    but perverseness therein is a breach in the spirit.

⁵ A fool despiseth his father's instruction:
    but he that regardeth reproof is prudent.

⁶ In the house of the righteous is much treasure:
    but in the revenues of the wicked is trouble.

⁷ The lips of the wise disperse knowledge:
    but the heart of the foolish doeth not so.

⁸ The sacrifice of the wicked
    is an abomination to the Lord:
        but the prayer of the upright is his delight.

⁹ The way of the wicked
    is an abomination unto the Lord:
        but he loveth him
    that followeth after righteousness.

¹⁰ Correction is grievous unto him
    that forsaketh the way:
        and he that hateth reproof shall die.

¹¹ Hell and destruction are before the Lord:
    how much more then
        the hearts of the children of men?

¹² A scorner loveth not one that reproveth him:
    neither will he go unto the wise.

¹³ A merry heart maketh a cheerful countenance:
    but by sorrow of the heart the spirit is broken.

¹⁴ The heart of him that hath understanding
    seeketh knowledge:
        but the mouth of fools feedeth on foolishness.

¹⁵ All the days of the afflicted are evil:
    but he that is of a merry heart
        hath a continual feast.

¹⁶ Better is little with the fear of the Lord
    than great treasure and trouble therewith.

¹⁷ Better is a dinner of herbs where love is,
    than a stalled ox and hatred therewith.

¹⁸ A wrathful man stirreth up strife:
    but he that is slow to anger appeaseth strife.

¹⁹ The way of the slothful man
    is as an hedge of thorns:
        but the way of the righteous is made plain.

²⁰ A wise son maketh a glad father:
    but a foolish man despiseth his mother.

²¹ Folly is joy to him that is destitute of wisdom:
    but a man of understanding walketh uprightly.

²² Without counsel purposes are disappointed:
    but in the multitude of counsellors
        they are established.

²³ A man hath joy by the answer of his mouth:
    and a word spoken in due season, how good is it!

²⁴ The way of life is above to the wise,
    that he may depart from hell beneath.

²⁵ The Lord will destroy the house of the proud:
    but he will establish the border of the widow.

²⁶ The thoughts of the wicked
    are an abomination to the Lord:
        but the words of the pure
    are pleasant words.

²⁷ He that is greedy of gain troubleth his own house:
    but he that hateth gifts shall live.

²⁸ The heart of the righteous studieth to answer:
    but the mouth of the wicked
        poureth out evil things.

²⁹ The Lord is far from the wicked:
    but he heareth the prayer of the righteous.

³⁰ The light of the eyes rejoiceth the heart:
    and a good report maketh the bones fat.

³¹ The ear that heareth the reproof of life
    abideth among the wise.

³² He that refuseth instruction
    despiseth his own soul:
        but he that heareth reproof
    getteth understanding.

³³ The fear of the Lord is the instruction of wisdom;
    and before honour is humility.

16 The preparations of the heart in man,
and the answer of the tongue, is from the Lord.

²All the ways of a man are clean in his own eyes;
but the Lord weigheth the spirits.

³Commit thy works unto the Lord,
and thy thoughts shall be established.

⁴The Lord hath made all things for himself:
yea, even the wicked for the day of evil.

⁵Every one that is proud in heart
is an abomination to the Lord:
though hand join in hand,
he shall not be unpunished.

⁶By mercy and truth iniquity is purged:
and by the fear of the Lord men depart from evil.

⁷When a man's ways please the Lord,
he maketh even his enemies
to be at peace with him.

⁸Better is a little with righteousness
than great revenues without right.

⁹A man's heart deviseth his way:
but the Lord directeth his steps.

[10]A divine sentence is in the lips of the king:
   his mouth transgresseth not in judgment.

[11]A just weight and balance are the Lord's:
   all the weights of the bag are his work.

[12]It is an abomination to kings to commit wickedness:
   for the throne is established by righteousness.

[13]Righteous lips are the delight of kings;
   and they love him that speaketh right.

[14]The wrath of a king is as messengers of death:
   but a wise man will pacify it.

[15]In the light of the king's countenance is life;
   and his favour is as a cloud of the latter rain.

[16]How much better is it to get wisdom than gold!
   And to get understanding
      rather to be chosen than silver!

[17]The highway of the upright is to depart from evil:
   he that keepeth his way preserveth his soul.

[18]Pride goeth before destruction,
   and an haughty spirit before a fall.

[19]Better it is to be of an humble spirit with the lowly,
   than to divide the spoil with the proud.

[20]He that handleth a matter wisely shall find good:
   and whoso trusteth in the Lord, happy is he.

²¹ The wise in heart shall be called prudent:
and the sweetness of the lips increaseth learning.

²² Understanding is a wellspring of life
unto him that hath it:
but the instruction of fools is folly.

²³ The heart of the wise teacheth his mouth,
and addeth learning to his lips.

²⁴ Pleasant words are as an honeycomb,
sweet to the soul, and health to the bones.

²⁵ There is a way that seemeth right unto a man,
but the end thereof are the ways of death.

²⁶ He that laboureth laboureth for himself:
for his mouth craveth it of him.

²⁷ An ungodly man diggeth up evil:
and in his lips there is as a burning fire.

²⁸ A froward man soweth strife,
and a whisperer separateth chief friends.

²⁹ A violent man enticeth his neighbour,
and leadeth him into the way that is not good.

³⁰ He shutteth his eyes to devise froward things:
moving his lips he bringeth evil to pass.

³¹ The hoary head is a crown of glory,
if it be found in the way of righteousness.

³² He that is slow to anger is better than the mighty;
and he that ruleth his spirit
than he that taketh a city.

³³ The lot is cast into the lap;
but the whole disposing thereof is of the Lord.

17 Better is a dry morsel, and quietness therewith,
than an house full of sacrifices with strife.

² A wise servant shall have rule over a son
that causeth shame,
and shall have part of the inheritance
among the brethren.

³ The fining pot is for silver, and the furnace for gold:
but the Lord trieth the hearts.

⁴ A wicked doer giveth heed to false lips;
and a liar giveth ear to a naughty tongue.

⁵ Whoso mocketh the poor reproacheth his Maker:
and he that is glad at calamities
shall not be unpunished.

⁶ Children's children are the crown of old men;
and the glory of children are their fathers.

⁷ Excellent speech becometh not a fool:
much less do lying lips a prince.

⁸A gift is as a precious stone
    in the eyes of him that hath it:
        whithersoever it turneth, it prospereth.

⁹He that covereth a transgression
    seeketh love;
        but he that repeateth a matter
    separateth very friends.

¹⁰A reproof entereth more into a wise man
    than an hundred stripes into a fool.

¹¹An evil man seeketh only rebellion:
    therefore a cruel messenger
        shall be sent against him.

¹²Let a bear robbed of her whelps meet a man,
    rather than a fool in his folly.

¹³Whoso rewardeth evil for good,
     evil shall not depart from his house.

¹⁴The beginning of strife
    is as when one letteth out water:
        therefore leave off contention,
    before it be meddled with.

¹⁵He that justifieth the wicked,
    and he that condemneth the just,
        even they both are
    abomination to the Lord.

¹⁶ Wherefore is there a price
in the hand of a fool to get wisdom,
seeing he hath no heart to it?

¹⁷ A friend loveth at all times,
and a brother is born for adversity.

¹⁸ A man void of understanding striketh hands,
and becometh surety
in the presence of his friend.

¹⁹ He loveth transgression that loveth strife:
and he that exalteth his gate seeketh destruction.

²⁰ He that hat a froward heart findeth no good:
and he that hath a perverse tongue
falleth into mischief.

²¹ He that begetteth a fool doeth it to his sorrow:
and the father of a fool hath no joy.

²² A merry heart doeth good like a medicine:
but a broken spirit drieth the bones.

²³ A wicked man taketh a gift out of the bosom
to pervert the ways of judgment.

²⁴ Wisdom is before him that hath understanding;
but the eyes of a fool are in the ends of the earth.

²⁵ A foolish son is a grief to his father,
and bitterness to her that bare him.

²⁶Also to punish the just is not good,
    nor to strike princes for equity.

²⁷ He that hath knowledge
    spareth his words:
        and a man of understanding
    is of an excellent spirit.

²⁸ Even a fool, when he holdeth his peace,
    is counted wise:
        and he that shutteth his lips
    is esteemed a man of understanding.

18 Through desire a man, having separated himself,
    seeketh and intermeddleth with all wisdom.

²A fool hath no delight in understanding,
    but that his heart may discover itself.

³ When the wicked cometh,
    then cometh also contempt,
        and with ignominy reproach.

⁴ The words of a man's mouth are as deep waters,
    and the wellspring of wisdom as a flowing brook.

⁵ It is not good to accept the person of the wicked,
    to overthrow the righteous in judgment.

⁶A fool's lips enter into contention,
    and his mouth calleth for strokes.

⁷A fool's mouth is his destruction,
and his lips are the snare of his soul.

⁸ The words of a tale-bearer are as wounds,
and they go down into
the innermost parts of the belly.

⁹ He also that is slothful in his work
is brother to him that is a great waster.

¹⁰ The name of the Lord is a strong tower:
the righteous runneth into it, and is safe.

¹¹ The rich man's wealth is his strong city,
and as an high wall in his own conceit.

¹² Before destruction the heart of man is haughty,
and before honour is humility.

¹³ He that answereth a matter before he heareth it,
it is folly and shame unto him.

¹⁴ The spirit of a man will sustain his infirmity;
but a wounded spirit who can bear?

¹⁵ The heart of the prudent getteth knowledge;
and the ear of the wise seeketh knowledge.

¹⁶ A man's gift maketh room for him,
and bringeth him before great men.

¹⁷ He that is first in his own cause seemeth just;
  but his neighbour cometh and searcheth him.

¹⁸ The lot causeth contentions to cease,
  and parteth between the mighty.

¹⁹ A brother offended is harder to be won
  than a strong city:
    and their contentions are like
  the bars of a castle.

²⁰ A man's belly shall be satisfied
  with the fruit of his mouth;
    and with the increase of his lips
  shall he be filled.

²¹ Death and life are in the power of the tongue:
  and they that love it
    shall eat the fruit thereof.

²² Whoso findeth a wife findeth a good thing,
  and obtaineth favour of the Lord.

²³ The poor useth intreaties;
  but the rich answereth roughly.

²⁴ A man that hath friends
  must shew himself friendly:
    and there is a friend
  that sticketh closer than a brother.

19 Better is the poor that walketh in his integrity,
than he that is perverse in his lips, and is a fool.

² Also, that the soul be without knowledge,
it is not good;
and he that hasteth with his feet sinneth.

³ The foolishness of man perverteth his way:
and his heart fretteth against the Lord.

⁴ Wealth maketh many friends;
but the poor is separated from his neighbour.

⁵ A false witness shall not be unpunished,
and he that speaketh lies shall not escape.

⁶ Many will intreat the favour of the prince:
and every man is a friend
to him that giveth gifts.

⁷ All the brethren of the poor do hate him:
how much more do his friends go far from him?
He pursueth them with words,
yet they are wanting to him.

⁸ He that getteth wisdom loveth his own soul;
he that keepeth understanding shall find good.

⁹ A false witness shall not be unpunished,
and he that speaketh lies shall perish.

¹⁰ Delight is not seemly for a fool;
much less for a servant to have rule over princes.

[11] The discretion of a man deferreth his anger;
   and it is his glory to pass over a transgression.

[12] The king's wrath is as the roaring of a lion;
   but his favour is as dew upon the grass.

[13] A foolish son is the calamity of his father:
   and the contentions of a wife
      are a continual dropping.

[14] House and riches are the inheritance of fathers:
   and a prudent wife is from the Lord.

[15] Slothfulness casteth into a deep sleep;
   and an idle soul shall suffer hunger.

[16] He that keepeth the commandment
   keepeth his own soul;
      but he that despiseth his ways shall die.

[17] He that hath pity upon the poor
   lendeth unto the Lord;
      and that which he hath given
   will he pay him again.

[18] Chasten thy son while there is hope,
   and let not thy soul spare for his crying.

[19] A man of great wrath shall suffer punishment:
   for if thou deliver him, yet thou must do it again.

[20] Hear counsel, and receive instruction,
   that thou mayest be wise in thy latter end.

²¹ There are many devices in a man's heart;
　　nevertheless the counsel of the Lord,
　　　　that shall stand.

²² The desire of a man is his kindness:
　　and a poor man is better than a liar.

²³ The fear of the Lord tendeth to life:
　　and he that hath it shall abide satisfied;
　　　　he shall not be visited with evil.

²⁴ A slothful man hideth his hand in his bosom,
　　and will not so much as
　　　　bring it to his mouth again.

²⁵ Smite a scorner, and the simple will beware:
　　and reprove one that hath understanding,
　　　　and he will understand knowledge.

²⁶ He that wasteth his father,
　　and chaseth away his mother,
　　　　is a son that causeth shame,
　　and bringeth reproach.

²⁷ Cease, my son, to hear the instruction
　　that causeth to err from the words of knowledge.

²⁸ An ungodly witness scorneth judgment:
　　and the mouth of the wicked devoureth iniquity.

²⁹ Judgments are prepared for scorners,
　　and stripes for the back of fools.

20 Wine is a mocker, strong drink is raging:
and whosoever is deceived thereby
is not wise.

² The fear of a king is as the roaring of a lion:
whoso provoketh him to anger
sinneth against his own soul.

³ It is an honour for a man to cease from strife:
but every fool will be meddling.

⁴ The sluggard will not plow by reason of the cold:
therefore shall he beg in harvest,
and have nothing.

⁵ Counsel in the heart of man is like deep water;
but a man of understanding will draw it out.

⁶ Most men will proclaim every one
his own goodness,
but a faithful man who can find?

⁷ The just man walketh in his integrity:
his children are blessed after him.

⁸ A king that sitteth in the throne of judgment
scattereth away all evil with his eyes.

⁹ Who can say, 'I have made my heart clean,
I am pure from my sin'?

¹⁰ Divers weights, and divers measures:
both of them are alike abomination to the Lord.

¹¹ Even a child is known by his doings,
>> whether his work be pure,
>>>> and whether it be right.

¹² The hearing ear, and the seeing eye,
>> the Lord hath made even both of them.

¹³ Love not sleep, lest thou come to poverty;
>> open thine eyes,
>>>> and thou shalt be satisfied with bread.

¹⁴ 'It is naught, it is naught,' saith the buyer,
>> but when he is gone his way, then he boasteth.

¹⁵ There is gold, and a multitude of rubies:
>> but the lips of knowledge are a precious jewel.

¹⁶ Take his garment that is surety for a stranger:
>> and take a pledge of him for a strange woman.

¹⁷ Bread of deceit is sweet to a man;
>> but afterwards his mouth shall be filled
>>>> with gravel.

¹⁸ Every purpose is established by counsel:
>> and with good advice make war.

¹⁹ He that goeth about as a tale-bearer
>> revealeth secrets:
>>>> therefore meddle not with him
>>>> that flattereth with his lips.

²⁰ Whoso curseth his father or his mother,
his lamp shall be put out in obscure darkness.

²¹ An inheritance may be gotten hastily
at the beginning;
but the end thereof shall not be blessed.

²² Say not thou, 'I will recompense evil';
but wait on the Lord, and he shall save thee.

²³ Divers weights are an abomination unto the Lord;
and a false balance is not good.

²⁴ Man's goings are of the Lord;
how can a man then understand his own way?

²⁵ It is a snare to the man who devoureth
that which is holy,
and after vows to make enquiry.

²⁶ A wise king scattereth the wicked,
and bringeth the wheel over them.

²⁷ The spirit of man is the candle of the Lord,
searching all the inward parts of the belly.

²⁸ Mercy and truth preserve the king:
and his throne is upholden by mercy.

²⁹ The glory of young men is their strength:
and the beauty of old men is the gray head.

³⁰ The blueness of a wound cleanseth away evil:
so do stripes the inward parts of the belly.

21 The king's heart is in the hand of the Lord,
as the rivers of water:
he turneth it whithersoever he will.

² Every way of a man is right in his own eyes:
but the Lord pondereth the hearts.

³ To do justice and judgment
is more acceptable to the Lord than sacrifice.

⁴ An high look, and a proud heart,
and the plowing of the wicked, is sin.

⁵ The thoughts of the diligent
tend only to plenteousness;
but of every one that is hasty only to want.

⁶ The getting of treasures
by a lying tongue is a vanity
tossed to and fro of them that seek death.

⁷ The robbery of the wicked shall destroy them;
because they refuse to do judgment.

⁸ The way of man is froward and strange:
but as for the pure, his work is right.

⁹ It is better to dwell in a corner of the housetop
than with a brawling woman in a wide house.

¹⁰ The soul of the wicked desireth evil:
   his neighbour findeth no favour in his eyes.

¹¹ When the scorner is punished,
   the simple is made wise:
      and when the wise is instructed,
   he receiveth knowledge.

¹² The righteous man wisely considereth
   the house of the wicked:
      but God overthroweth the wicked
   for their wickedness.

¹³ Whoso stoppeth his ears at the cry of the poor,
   he also shall cry himself, but shall not be heard.

¹⁴ A gift in secret pacifieth anger:
   and a reward in the bosom strong wrath.

¹⁵ It is joy to the just to do judgment:
   but destruction shall be
      to the workers of iniquity.

¹⁶ The man that wandereth
   out of the way of understanding
      shall remain in the congregation of the dead.

¹⁷ He that loveth pleasure shall be a poor man:
   he that loveth wine and oil shall not be rich.

¹⁸ The wicked shall be a ransom for the righteous,
   and the transgressor for the upright.

¹⁹ It is better to dwell in the wilderness,
　　than with a contentious and an angry woman.

²⁰ There is treasure to be desired
　　and oil in the dwelling of the wise;
　　　　but a foolish man spendeth it up.

²¹ He that followeth after righteousness and mercy
　　findeth life, righteousness, and honour.

²² A wise man scaleth the city of the mighty,
　　and casteth down the strength
　　　　of the confidence thereof.

²³ Whoso keepeth his mouth and his tongue
　　keepeth his soul from troubles.

²⁴ Proud and haughty scorner is his name,
　　who dealeth in proud wrath.

²⁵ The desire of the slothful killeth him,
　　for his hands refuse to labour.
²⁶ He coveteth greedily all the day long,
　　but the righteous giveth and spareth not.

²⁷ The sacrifice of the wicked is abomination:
　　how much more,
　　　　when he bringeth it with a wicked mind?

²⁸ A false witness shall perish:
　　but the man that heareth speaketh constantly.

²⁹A wicked man hardeneth his face:
   but as for the upright, he directeth his way.

³⁰There is no wisdom nor understanding
   nor counsel against the Lord.

³¹The horse is prepared against the day of battle:
   but safety is of the Lord.

22 A good name is rather to be chosen
      than great riches,
         and loving favour
      rather than silver and gold.

²The rich and poor meet together:
   the Lord is the maker of them all.

³A prudent man foreseeth the evil,
   and hideth himself:
      but the simple pass on,
   and are punished.

⁴By humility and the fear of the Lord are riches,
   and honour, and life.

⁵Thorns and snares are in the way of the froward:
   he that doth keep his soul shall be far from them.

⁶Train up a child in the way he should go:
   and when he is old, he will not depart from it.

⁷ The rich ruleth over the poor,
   and the borrower is servant to the lender.

⁸ He that soweth iniquity shall reap vanity:
   and the rod of his anger shall fail.

⁹ He that hath a bountiful eye shall be blessed;
   for he giveth of his bread to the poor.

¹⁰ Cast out the scorner, and contention shall go out;
   yea, strife and reproach shall cease.

¹¹ He that loveth pureness of heart,
   for the grace of his lips
      the king shall be his friend.

¹² The eyes of the Lord preserve knowledge,
   and he overthroweth the words
      of the transgressor.

¹³ The slothful man saith,
   'There is a lion without,
      I shall be slain in the streets.'

¹⁴ The mouth of strange women is a deep pit:
   he that is abhorred of the Lord shall fall therein.

¹⁵ Foolishness is bound in the heart of a child;
   but the rod of correction
      shall drive it far from him.

[16] He that oppresseth the poor to increase his riches,
    and he that giveth to the rich,
        shall surely come to want.

[17] Bow down thine ear, and hear the words of the wise,
    and apply thine heart unto my knowledge.
[18] For it is a pleasant thing
    if thou keep them within thee;
        they shall withal be fitted in thy lips.
[19] That thy trust may be in the Lord,
    I have made known to thee this day, even to thee.

[20] Have not I written to thee excellent things
    in counsels and knowledge,
[21] that I might make thee know the certainty
    of the words of truth;
        that thou mightest answer the words of truth
    to them that send unto thee?

[22] Rob not the poor, because he is poor:
    neither oppress the afflicted in the gate:
[23] for the Lord will plead their cause,
    and spoil the soul of those that spoiled them.

[24] Make no friendship with an angry man;
    and with a furious man thou shalt not go:
[25] lest thou learn his ways,
    and get a snare to thy soul.

²⁶ Be not thou one of them that strike hands,
   or of them that are sureties for debts.
²⁷ If thou hast nothing to pay,
   why should he take away thy bed
      from under thee?

²⁸ Remove not the ancient landmark,
   which thy fathers have set.

²⁹ Seest thou a man diligent in his business?
   He shall stand before kings;
      he shall not stand before mean men.

23 When thou sittest to eat with a ruler,
   consider diligently what is before thee:
² and put a knife to thy throat,
   if thou be a man given to appetite.
³ Be not desirous of his dainties:
   for they are deceitful meat.

⁴ Labour not to be rich:
   cease from thine own wisdom.
⁵ Wilt thou set thine eyes upon that which is not?
   For riches certainly make themselves wings;
      they fly away as an eagle toward heaven.

⁶ Eat thou not the bread of him that hath an evil eye,
   neither desire thou his dainty meats:

⁷for as he thinketh in his heart, so is he.
'Eat and drink,' saith he to thee;
but his heart is not with thee.
⁸ The morsel which thou hast eaten
shalt thou vomit up,
and lose thy sweet words.

⁹ Speak not in the ears of a fool:
for he will despise
the wisdom of thy words.

¹⁰ Remove not the old landmark;
and enter not into the fields of the fatherless:
¹¹ for their redeemer is mighty;
he shall plead their cause with thee.

¹²Apply thine heart unto instruction,
and thine ears to the words of knowledge.

¹³ Withhold not correction from the child:
for if thou beatest him with the rod,
he shall not die.
¹⁴ Thou shalt beat him with the rod,
and shalt deliver his soul from hell.

¹⁵ My son, if thine heart be wise,
my heart shall rejoice, even mine.
¹⁶ Yea, my reins shall rejoice,
when thy lips speak right things.

[17] Let not thine heart envy sinners:
  but be thou in the fear of the Lord
    all the day long.
[18] For surely there is an end;
  and thine expectation shall not be cut off.

[19] Hear thou, my son, and be wise,
  and guide thine heart in the way.
[20] Be not among winebibbers;
  among riotous eaters of flesh:
[21] for the drunkard and the glutton
  shall come to poverty:
    and drowsiness shall clothe a man with rags.

[22] Hearken unto thy father that begat thee,
  and despise not thy mother when she is old.
[23] Buy the truth, and sell it not; also wisdom,
  and instruction, and understanding.
[24] The father of the righteous shall greatly rejoice:
  and he that begetteth a wise child
    shall have joy of him.
[25] Thy father and thy mother shall be glad,
  and she that bare thee shall rejoice.

[26] My son, give me thine heart,
  and let thine eyes observe my ways.
[27] For a whore is a deep ditch;
  and a strange woman is a narrow pit.

²⁸ She also lieth in wait as for a prey,
    and increaseth the transgressors among men.

²⁹ Who hath woe? Who hath sorrow?
    Who hath contentions? Who hath babbling?
      Who hath wounds without cause?
    Who hath redness of eyes?
³⁰ They that tarry long at the wine,
    they that go to seek mixed wine.
³¹ Look not thou upon the wine when it is red,
    when it giveth his colour in the cup,
      when it moveth itself aright.
³² At the last it biteth like a serpent,
    and stingeth like an adder.
³³ Thine eyes shall behold strange women,
    and thine heart shall utter perverse things.
³⁴ Yea, thou shalt be as he that lieth down
    in the midst of the sea,
      or as he that lieth upon the top of a mast.
³⁵ 'They have stricken me,' shalt thou say,
    'and I was not sick;
      they have beaten me, and I felt it not.
    When shall I awake? I will seek it yet again.'

24 Be not thou envious against evil men,
neither desire to be with them.
² For their heart studieth destruction,
and their lips talk of mischief.

³ Through wisdom is an house builded;
and by understanding it is established:
⁴ and by knowledge shall the chambers be filled
with all precious and pleasant riches.

⁵ A wise man is strong;
yea, a man of knowledge increaseth strength.
⁶ For by wise counsel thou shalt make thy war:
and in multitude of counsellors
there is safety.

⁷ Wisdom is too high for a fool:
he openeth not his mouth in the gate.

⁸ He that deviseth to do evil
shall be called a mischievous person.
⁹ The thought of foolishness is sin:
and the scorner is an abomination to men.

¹⁰ If thou faint in the day of adversity,
thy strength is small.
¹¹ If thou forbear to deliver
them that are drawn unto death,
and those that are ready to be slain;

¹² if thou sayest, 'Behold, we knew it not,'
    doth not he that pondereth the heart consider it?
        And he that keepeth thy soul,
    doth not he know it?
        And shall not he render to every man
    according to his works?

¹³ My son, eat thou honey, because it is good;
    and the honeycomb, which is sweet to thy taste:
¹⁴ so shall the knowledge of wisdom be unto thy soul:
    when thou hast found it,
        then there shall be a reward,
    and thy expectation shall not be cut off.

¹⁵ Lay not wait, O wicked man,
    against the dwelling of the righteous;
        spoil not his resting place:
¹⁶ for a just man falleth seven times,
    and riseth up again:
        but the wicked shall fall into mischief.

¹⁷ Rejoice not when thine enemy falleth,
    and let not thine heart be glad
        when he stumbleth:
¹⁸ lest the Lord see it, and it displease him,
    and he turn away his wrath from him.

¹⁹ Fret not thyself because of evil men,
    neither be thou envious at the wicked;

²⁰ for there shall be no reward to the evil man;
   the candle of the wicked shall be put out.

²¹ My son, fear thou the Lord and the king,
   and meddle not with them
      that are given to change:
²² for their calamity shall rise suddenly;
   and who knoweth the ruin of them both?

²³ These things also belong to the wise.

   It is not good to have respect of persons in judgment.
²⁴ He that saith unto the wicked,
      'Thou art righteous,' him shall the people curse,
         nations shall abhor him:
²⁵ but to them that rebuke him shall be delight,
   and a good blessing shall come upon them.
²⁶ Every man shall kiss his lips
   that giveth a right answer.

²⁷ Prepare thy work without,
   and make it fit for thyself in the field;
      and afterwards build thine house.

²⁸ Be not a witness against thy neighbour
   without cause;
      and deceive not with thy lips.
²⁹ Say not, 'I will do so to him as he hath done to me:
   I will render to the man according to his work.'

³⁰ I went by the field of the slothful,
and by the vineyard of the man
void of understanding;
³¹ and, lo, it was all grown over with thorns,
and nettles had covered the face thereof,
and the stone wall thereof was broken down.
³² Then I saw, and considered it well:
I looked upon it,
and received instruction.
³³ Yet a little sleep, a little slumber,
a little folding of the hands to sleep:
³⁴ so shall thy poverty come as one that travelleth;
and thy want as an armed man.

25 These are also proverbs of Solomon, which the men of
Hezekiah king of Judah copied out.

² It is the glory of God to conceal a thing:
but the honour of kings is to search out a matter.
³ The heaven for height, and the earth for depth,
and the heart of kings is unsearchable.

⁴ Take away the dross from the silver,
and there shall come forth a vessel for the finer.
⁵ Take away the wicked from before the king,
and his throne shall be established
in righteousness.

⁶ Put not forth thyself in the presence of the king,
   and stand not in the place of great men:
⁷ for better it is that it be said unto thee,
   'Come up hither,' than that thou shouldest be put
      lower in the presence of the prince
   whom thine eyes have seen.

⁸ Go not forth hastily to strive,
   lest thou know not what to do in the end thereof,
      when thy neighbour hath put thee to shame.

⁹ Debate thy cause with thy neighbour himself;
   and discover not a secret to another:
¹⁰ lest he that heareth it put thee to shame,
   and thine infamy turn not away.

¹¹ A word fitly spoken is like apples of gold
   in pictures of silver.
¹² As an earring of gold, and an ornament of fine gold,
   so is a wise reprover upon an obedient ear.

¹³ As the cold of snow in the time of harvest,
   so is a faithful messenger to them that send him:
      for he refresheth the soul of his masters.

¹⁴ Whoso boasteth himself of a false gift
   is like clouds and wind without rain.

¹⁵ By long forbearing is a prince persuaded,
   and a soft tongue breaketh the bone.

¹⁶ Hast thou found honey?
Eat so much as is sufficient for thee,
lest thou be filled therewith, and vomit it.

¹⁷ Withdraw thy foot from thy neighbour's house;
lest he be weary of thee, and so hate thee.

¹⁸ A man that beareth false witness
against his neighbour
is a maul, and a sword, and a sharp arrow.

¹⁹ Confidence in an unfaithful man in time of trouble
is like a broken tooth, and a foot out of joint.

²⁰ As he that taketh away a garment in cold weather,
and as vinegar upon nitre,
so is he that singeth songs to an heavy heart.

²¹ If thine enemy be hungry, give him bread to eat;
and if he be thirsty, give him water to drink:
²² for thou shalt heap coals of fire upon his head,
and the Lord shall reward thee.

²³ The north wind driveth away rain:
so doth an angry countenance
a backbiting tongue.

²⁴ It is better to dwell in the corner of the housetop,
than with a brawling woman
and in a wide house.

²⁵As cold waters to a thirsty soul,
  so is good news from a far country.

²⁶A righteous man falling down before the wicked
  is as a troubled fountain, and a corrupt spring.

²⁷It is not good to eat much honey:
  so for men to search their own glory is not glory.

²⁸He that hath no rule over his own spirit
  is like a city that is broken down,
    and without walls.

26 As snow in summer, and as rain in harvest,
  so honour is not seemly for a fool.

²As the bird by wandering, as the swallow by flying,
  so the curse causeless shall not come.

³A whip for the horse, a bridle for the ass,
  and a rod for the fool's back.

⁴Answer not a fool according to his folly,
  lest thou also be like unto him.

⁵Answer a fool according to his folly,
  lest he be wise in his own conceit.

⁶He that sendeth a message by the hand of a fool
  cutteth off the feet, and drinketh damage.

[7] The legs of the lame are not equal:
　　　so is a parable in the mouth of fools.

[8] As he that bindeth a stone in a sling,
　　　so is he that giveth honour to a fool.

[9] As a thorn goeth up into the hand of a drunkard,
　　　so is a parable in the mouth of fools.

[10] The great God that formed all things
　　　both rewardeth the fool,
　　　　　and rewardeth transgressors.

[11] As a dog returneth to his vomit,
　　　so a fool returneth to his folly.

[12] Seest thou a man wise in his own conceit?
　　　There is more hope of a fool than of him.

[13] The slothful man saith,
　　　'There is a lion in the way;
　　　　　a lion is in the streets.'

[14] As the door turneth upon his hinges,
　　　so doth the slothful upon his bed.

[15] The slothful hideth his hand in his bosom;
　　　it grieveth him to bring it again to his mouth.

[16] The sluggard is wiser in his own conceit
　　　than seven men that can render a reason.

¹⁷ He that passeth by, and meddleth with strife
        belonging not to him,
                is like one that taketh a dog by the ears.

¹⁸ As a mad man who casteth firebrands,
        arrows, and death,
¹⁹ so is the man that deceiveth his neighbour,
        and saith, 'Am not I in sport?'

²⁰ Where no wood is, there the fire goeth out:
        so where there is no talebearer,
                the strife ceaseth.

²¹ As coals are to burning coals, and wood to fire;
        so is a contentious man to kindle strife.

²² The words of a talebearer are as wounds,
        and they go down
                into the innermost parts of the belly.
²³ Burning lips and a wicked heart
        are like a potsherd covered with silver dross.

²⁴ He that hateth dissembleth with his lips,
        and layeth up deceit within him;
²⁵ when he speaketh fair, believe him not:
        for there are seven abominations in his heart.
²⁶ Whose hatred is covered by deceit,
        his wickedness shall be shewed
                before the whole congregation.

²⁷ Whoso diggeth a pit shall fall therein:
    and he that rolleth a stone,
        it will return upon him.

²⁸A lying tongue hateth those that are afflicted by it;
    and a flattering mouth worketh ruin.

27 Boast not thyself of tomorrow;
    for thou knowest not what a day may bring forth.

² Let another man praise thee,
    and not thine own mouth;
        a stranger, and not thine own lips.

³A stone is heavy, and the sand weighty;
    but a fool's wrath is heavier than them both.

⁴Wrath is cruel, and anger is outrageous;
    but who is able to stand before envy?

⁵Open rebuke is better than secret love.

⁶Faithful are the wounds of a friend;
    but the kisses of an enemy are deceitful.

⁷The full soul loatheth an honeycomb;
    but to the hungry soul every bitter thing is sweet.

⁸As a bird that wandereth from her nest,
    so is a man that wandereth from his place.

⁹ Ointment and perfume rejoice the heart:
    so doth the sweetness of a man's friend
      by hearty counsel.

¹⁰ Thine own friend, and thy father's friend,
    forsake not;
      neither go into thy brother's house
    in the day of thy calamity:
      for better is a neighbour
    that is near than a brother far off.

¹¹ My son, be wise, and make my heart glad,
    that I may answer him that reproacheth me.

¹² A prudent man foreseeth the evil, and hideth himself;
    but the simple pass on, and are punished.

¹³ Take his garment that is surety for a stranger,
    and take a pledge of him for a strange woman.

¹⁴ He that blesseth his friend with a loud voice,
    rising early in the morning,
      it shall be counted a curse to him.

¹⁵ A continual dropping in a very rainy day
    and a contentious woman are alike.
¹⁶ Whosoever hideth her hideth the wind,
    and the ointment of his right hand,
      which bewrayeth itself.

¹⁷ Iron sharpeneth iron; so a man sharpeneth
    the countenance of his friend.

¹⁸ Whoso keepeth the fig tree shall eat the fruit thereof:
    so he that waiteth on his master shall be honoured.

¹⁹ As in water face answereth to face,
    so the heart of man to man.

²⁰ Hell and destruction are never full;
    so the eyes of man are never satisfied.

²¹ As the fining pot for silver,
    and the furnace for gold;
        so is a man to his praise.

²² Though thou shouldest bray a fool in a mortar
    among wheat with a pestle,
        yet will not his foolishness depart from him.

²³ Be thou diligent to know the state of thy flocks,
    and look well to thy herds.
²⁴ For riches are not for ever:
    and doth the crown endure to every generation?
²⁵ The hay appeareth,
    and the tender grass sheweth itself,
        and herbs of the mountains are gathered.
²⁶ The lambs are for thy clothing,
    and the goats are the price of the field.

²⁷And thou shalt have goats' milk enough
  for thy food, for the food of thy household,
    and for the maintenance for thy maidens.

28 The wicked flee when no man pursueth:
    but the righteous are bold as a lion.

²For the transgression of a land
  many are the princes thereof,
    but by a man of understanding and knowledge
  the state thereof shall be prolonged.

³A poor man that oppresseth the poor
  is like a sweeping rain which leaveth no food.

⁴They that forsake the law praise the wicked:
  but such as keep the law contend with them.

⁵Evil men understand not judgment:
  but they that seek the
    Lord understand all things.

⁶Better is the poor that walketh in his uprightness,
  than he that is perverse in his ways,
    though he be rich.

⁷Whoso keepeth the law is a wise son:
  but he that is a companion of riotous men
    shameth his father.

⁸ He that by usury and unjust gain
   increaseth his substance,
      he shall gather it for him
   that will pity the poor.

⁹ He that turneth away his ear from hearing the law,
   even his prayer shall be abomination.

¹⁰ Whoso causeth the righteous to go astray
   in an evil way,
      he shall fall himself into his own pit:
   but the upright shall have good things
      in possession.

¹¹ The rich man is wise in his own conceit;
   but the poor that hath understanding
      searcheth him out.

¹² When righteous men do rejoice,
   there is great glory:
      but when the wicked rise, a man is hidden.

¹³ He that covereth his sins shall not prosper:
   but whoso confesseth and forsaketh them
      shall have mercy.

¹⁴ Happy is the man that feareth alway:
   but he that hardeneth his heart
      shall fall into mischief.

¹⁵As a roaring lion, and a ranging bear;
   so is a wicked ruler over the poor people.

¹⁶ The prince that wanteth understanding
   is also a great oppressor:
         but he that hateth covetousness
   shall prolong his days.

¹⁷A man that doeth violence
   to the blood of any person
         shall flee to the pit;
   let no man stay him.

¹⁸ Whoso walketh uprightly shall be saved,
   but he that is perverse in his ways
         shall fall at once.

¹⁹ He that tilleth his land
   shall have plenty of bread:
         but he that followeth after vain persons
   shall have poverty enough.

²⁰A faithful man shall abound with blessings:
   but he that maketh haste to be rich
         shall not be innocent.

²¹ To have respect of persons is not good,
   for for a piece of bread that man will transgress.

²² He that hasteth to be rich hath an evil eye,
   and considereth not
         that poverty shall come upon him.

²³ He that rebuketh a man
　　afterwards shall find more favour
　　　　than he that flattereth with the tongue.

²⁴ Whoso robbeth his father or his mother, and saith,
　　'It is no transgression,'
　　　　the same is the companion of a destroyer.

²⁵ He that is of a proud heart stirreth up strife:
　　but he that putteth his trust in the Lord
　　　　shall be made fat.

²⁶ He that trusteth in his own heart is a fool:
　　but whoso walketh wisely, he shall be delivered.

²⁷ He that giveth unto the poor shall not lack:
　　but he that hideth his eyes
　　　　shall have many a curse.

²⁸ When the wicked rise, men hide themselves:
　　but when they perish, the righteous increase.

29

He, that being often reproved, hardeneth his neck,
　　shall suddenly be destroyed,
　　　　and that without remedy.

² When the righteous are in authority,
　　the people rejoice:
　　　　but when the wicked beareth rule,
　　the people mourn.

³ Whoso loveth wisdom rejoiceth his father:
   but he that keepeth company with harlots
      spendeth his substance.

⁴ The king by judgment establisheth the land:
   but he that receiveth gifts overthroweth it.

⁵ A man that flattereth his neighbour
   spreadeth a net for his feet.

⁶ In the transgression of an evil man there is a snare:
   but the righteous doth sing and rejoice.

⁷ The righteous considereth the cause of the poor:
   but the wicked regardeth not to know it.

⁸ Scornful men bring a city into a snare:
   but wise men turn away wrath.

⁹ If a wise man contendeth with a foolish man,
   whether he rage or laugh, there is no rest.

¹⁰ The bloodthirsty hate the upright:
   but the just seek his soul.

¹¹ A fool uttereth all his mind:
   but a wise man keepeth it in till afterwards.

¹² If a ruler hearken to lies,
   all his servants are wicked.

¹³ The poor and the deceitful man meet together:
   the Lord lighteneth both their eyes.

¹⁴The king that faithfully judgeth the poor,
   his throne shall be established for ever.

¹⁵The rod and reproof give wisdom:
   but a child left to himself
      bringeth his mother to shame.

¹⁶When the wicked are multiplied,
   transgression increaseth:
      but the righteous shall see their fall.

¹⁷Correct thy son, and he shall give thee rest;
   yea, he shall give delight unto thy soul.

¹⁸Where there is no vision, the people perish:
   but he that keepeth the law, happy is he.

¹⁹A servant will not be corrected by words:
   for though he understand he will not answer.

²⁰Seest thou a man that is hasty in his words?
   There is more hope of a fool than of him.

²¹He that delicately bringeth up
   his servant from a child
      shall have him become his son at the length.

²²An angry man stirreth up strife,
   and a furious man aboundeth in transgression.

²³A man's pride shall bring him low:
   but honour shall uphold the humble in spirit.

²⁴ Whoso is partner with a thief hateth his own soul:
   he heareth cursing, and bewrayeth it not.

²⁵ The fear of man bringeth a snare:
   but whoso putteth his trust in the Lord
      shall be safe.

²⁶ Many seek the ruler's favour;
   but every man's judgment
      cometh from the Lord.

²⁷ An unjust man is an abomination to the just:
   and he that is upright in the way
      is abomination to the wicked.

30 The words of Agur the son of Jakeh, even the prophecy:
   the man spake unto Ithiel, even unto Ithiel and Ucal,

² 'Surely I am more brutish than any man,
   and have not the understanding of a man.
³ I neither learned wisdom,
   nor have the knowledge of the holy.
⁴ Who hath ascended up into heaven, or descended?
   Who hath gathered the wind in his fists?
      Who hath bound the waters in a garment?
   Who hath established all the ends of the earth?
      What is his name, and what is his son's name,
         if thou canst tell?

⁵ 'Every word of God is pure;
    he is a shield unto them
        that put their trust in him.
⁶ Add thou not unto his words,
    lest he reprove thee, and thou be found a liar.

⁷ 'Two things have I required of thee;
    deny me them not before I die:
⁸ remove far from me vanity and lies:
    give me neither poverty nor riches;
        feed me with food convenient for me:
⁹ lest I be full, and deny thee, and say,
    "Who is the Lord?" or lest I be poor, and steal,
        and take the name of my God in vain.

¹⁰ 'Accuse not a servant unto his master,
    lest he curse thee, and thou be found guilty.

¹¹ 'There is a generation that curseth their father,
    and doth not bless their mother.
¹² There is a generation that are pure in their own eyes,
    and yet is not washed from their filthiness.
¹³ There is a generation, O how lofty are their eyes!
    And their eyelids are lifted up.
¹⁴ There is a generation, whose teeth are as swords,
    and their jaw teeth as knives,
        to devour the poor from off the earth,
    and the needy from among men.

¹⁵ 'The horseleach hath two daughters, crying,
  "Give, give."

  There are three things that are never satisfied,
      yea, four things say not, "It is enough."
¹⁶ The grave; and the barren womb;
    the earth that is not filled with water;
        and the fire that saith not, "It is enough."

¹⁷ 'The eye that mocketh at his father,
    and despiseth to obey his mother,
        the ravens of the valley shall pick it out,
    and the young eagles shall eat it.

¹⁸ There be three things which are too wonderful for me,
      yea, four which I know not:
¹⁹ the way of an eagle in the air;
    the way of a serpent upon a rock;
        the way of a ship in the midst of the sea;
    and the way of a man with a maid.

²⁰ 'Such is the way of an adulterous woman;
    she eateth, and wipeth her mouth, and saith,
        "I have done no wickedness."

²¹ 'For three things the earth is disquieted,
    and for four which it cannot bear:
²² for a servant when he reigneth;
    and a fool when he is filled with meat;

²³ for an odious woman when she is married;
   and an handmaid that is heir to her mistress.

²⁴ 'There be four things
   which are little upon the earth,
      but they are exceeding wise:
²⁵ the ants are a people not strong,
   yet they prepare their meat in the summer;
²⁶ the conies are but a feeble folk,
   yet make they their houses in the rocks;
²⁷ the locusts have no king,
   yet go they forth all of them by bands;
²⁸ the spider taketh hold with her hands,
   and is in kings' palaces.

²⁹ There be three things which go well,
   yea, four are comely in going:
³⁰ a lion which is strongest among beasts,
   and turneth not away for any;
³¹ a greyhound; an he-goat also;
   and a king, against whom there is no rising up.

³² If thou hast done foolishly in lifting up thyself,
   or if thou hast thought evil,
      lay thine hand upon thy mouth.
³³ Surely the churning of milk bringeth forth butter,
   and the wringing of the nose bringeth forth blood:
      so the forcing of wrath bringeth forth strife.'

31

The words of king Lemuel, the prophecy that his mother taught him.

² What, my son? And what, the son of my womb?
  And what, the son of my vows?
³ Give not thy strength unto women,
  nor thy ways to that which destroyeth kings.

⁴ It is not for kings, O Lemuel,
  it is not for kings to drink wine;
    nor for princes strong drink:
⁵ lest they drink, and forget the law,
  and pervert the judgment of any of the afflicted.
⁶ Give strong drink unto him that is ready to perish,
  and wine unto those that be of heavy hearts.
⁷ Let him drink, and forget his poverty,
  and remember his misery no more.

⁸ Open thy mouth for the dumb
  in the cause of all
    such as are appointed to destruction.
⁹ Open thy mouth, judge righteously,
  and plead the cause of the poor and needy.

¹⁰ Who can find a virtuous woman?
  For her price is far above rubies.
¹¹ The heart of her husband
  doth safely trust in her,
    so that he shall have no need of spoil.

¹² She will do him good and not evil
  all the days of her life.
¹³ She seeketh wool, and flax,
  and worketh willingly with her hands.
¹⁴ She is like the merchants' ships;
  she bringeth her food from afar.
¹⁵ She riseth also while it is yet night,
  and giveth meat to her household,
    and a portion to her maidens.
¹⁶ She considereth a field, and buyeth it:
  with the fruit of her hands
    she planteth a vineyard.
¹⁷ She girdeth her loins with strength,
  and strengtheneth her arms.
¹⁸ She perceiveth that her merchandise is good:
  her candle goeth not out by night.
¹⁹ She layeth her hands to the spindle,
  and her hands hold the distaff.
²⁰ She stretcheth out her hand to the poor;
  yea, she reacheth forth her hands to the needy.
²¹ She is not afraid of the snow for her household:
  for all her household are clothed with scarlet.
²² She maketh herself coverings of tapestry;
  her clothing is silk and purple.
²³ Her husband is known in the gates,
  when he sitteth among the elders of the land.
²⁴ She maketh fine linen, and selleth it;

and delivereth girdles unto the merchant.
²⁵ Strength and honour are her clothing;
    and she shall rejoice in time to come.
²⁶ She openeth her mouth with wisdom;
    and in her tongue is the law of kindness.
²⁷ She looketh well to the ways of her household,
    and eateth not the bread of idleness.
²⁸ Her children arise up, and call her blessed;
    her husband also, and he praiseth her.
²⁹ Many daughters have done virtuously,
    but thou excellest them all.
³⁰ Favour is deceitful, and beauty is vain:
    but a woman that feareth the Lord,
        she shall be praised.
³¹ Give her of the fruit of her hands;
    and let her own works praise her in the gates.

titles in the series